PUZZLE MASTERS

COLOR QUEST

COLOR BY NUMBERS

BARRON'S

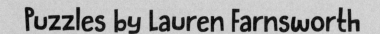

Puzzles by Lauren Farnsworth

Edited by Imogen Williams
Text by Amanda Learmonth
Designed by Derrian Bradder
Cover designed by Angie Allison and John Bigwood

First edition for the United States, its territories and dependencies, and
Canada published in 2018 by Barron's Educational Series, Inc.

Published in Great Britain in 2018 by Buster Books,
an imprint of Michael O'Mara Books Limited,
9 Lion Yard, Tremadoc Road, London SW4 7NQ

All inquiries should be addressed to:
Barron's Educational Series, Inc.
250 Wireless Boulevard
Hauppauge, NY 11788
www.barronseduc.com

ISBN: 978-1-4380-1146-2

Date of manufacture: January 2018
Manufactured by: W06K06T

Printed in China
9 8 7 6 5 4 3 2 1

INTRODUCTION

Are you ready for the ultimate
puzzle challenge?

This book is packed with extreme coloring
puzzles—complete each one to reveal a
hidden picture. Each page can be pulled out
and displayed when you have finished.

Each puzzle is a numbered pattern. Color in
the numbered spaces by following the color code that
appears on the opposite page. If there isn't a number in
a space, leave it white. Gradually, a picture will be revealed.

Don't worry if you don't have pens and pencils in exactly the same
shade as the colors shown. Get creative—make darker shades by
pressing harder and blend colors together if you need to.

Beside each puzzle you will find four riddle-styled clues
to help you guess what picture you are going to reveal,
with space underneath to write your answer.

Why not fill in how long each puzzle takes you to complete
in the space provided at the bottom of the page?

The finished images and answers are
all at the back of the book.

FUNNY FISH

I am a type of fish. You'll find me swimming in the warm shallow waters of the Indian and Pacific Oceans.

I often hide among sea anemones. Their poisonous tentacles, which don't sting me, protect me from hungry predators.

I am named for my brightly colored stripes, and for the funny, wobbly way I swim.

I feed on tiny sea animals, called zooplankton, and small plants. I also keep sea anemones clean by picking harmful parasites from their tentacles.

WHAT AM I?

....

1
2
3
4
5
6
7
8
9
10
11
12
13

TIME: ....

NIGHT HUNTER

If you're lucky, you might spot me at dusk, swooping silently through the air in search of prey.

I am known for my wide-eyed stare and huge eyes at the front of my head. I also have a sharp, hooked beak.

Although my eyesight is excellent, I can't actually move my eyes. To look around, I can move my entire head almost in a full circle.

When hunting on a dark night, I use my super-sharp hearing to locate my prey. I can hear a mouse move from 70 feet (20 m) away.

WHAT AM I?

....

TIME: ....

131 | 1
21 | 2
197 | 3
155
155 | 4
148 / 155 | 5
113 | 6
145 | 7
43 | 8
126 | 9
102 | 10
276 | 11
95 | 12
290 | 13
162 | 14
224 | 15

FAR, FAR AWAY

As the second largest planet in the Solar System, I am so huge you could fit 764 Earths inside of me.

I lie billions of miles from Earth, but can still be seen in the night sky as a bright point of light.

I am named after the Roman god of agriculture. There is also a day of the week that sounds like my name.

I am most well known for the huge rings of ice crystals and dust that surround me.

WHAT AM I?

....

TIME: ....

4
5
6
7
8
9
10
11

NIBBLE AND GNAW

My slim, bendy body is perfect for running, jumping, and climbing among the treetops.

I love to nibble on nuts and seeds. My four front teeth don't wear down from all the gnawing because they never stop growing.

Some of my species live on the ground. They collect nuts, fruit, and seeds in their cheek pouches to store in burrows over the winter.

You'll find me in all kinds of habitats, from rainforests and woodlands to deserts and bush.

WHAT AM I?

....

TIME: ....

1
2
3
4
5
6
7
8
9
10
11
12
13
14

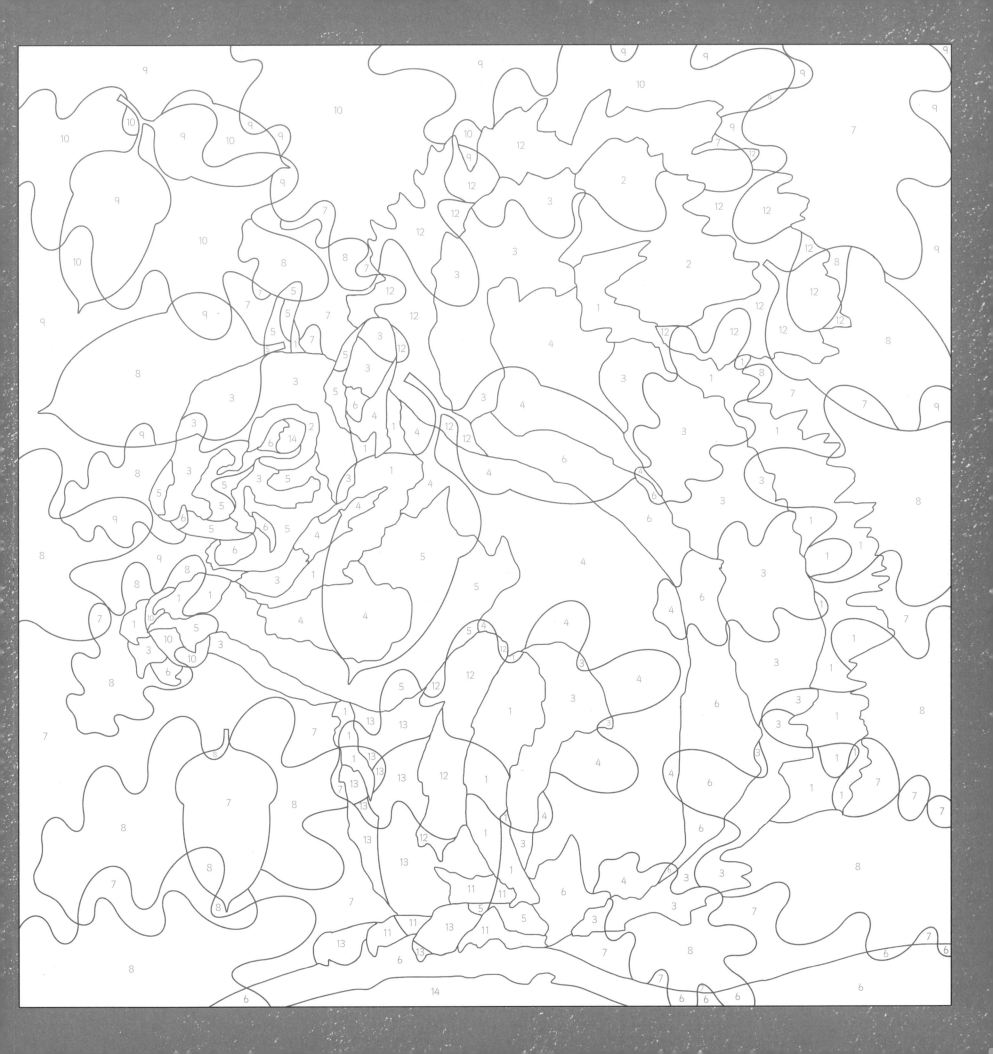

CLEVER CRITTER

1
2
3
4
5
6
7
8
9
10
11
12
13

With my large brain, I'm a clever creature. I have been known to use my long arms to unscrew the lid of a jar to get at the food inside.

I have long, powerful arms with rows of cup-shaped suckers. These help me to catch my prey and grip onto rocks on the seabed.

I live in seas and oceans around the world and belong to a group of animals called mollusks.

If another sea creature tries to attack me, I blast a cloud of black ink in its face to confuse it.

WHAT AM I?

....

TIME: ....

PRETTY IN PINK

I get my coloring from a diet of shrimp and algae. They contain chemicals that turn my feathers pink.

My stilt-like legs are really long. They keep me dry as I wade through the water in search of food.

I spend most of my day with my head upside down, filtering food from the water through my curved beak.

I live in large flocks of thousands of birds in lakes and lagoons around the world.

224

WHAT AM I?

....

TIME: ....

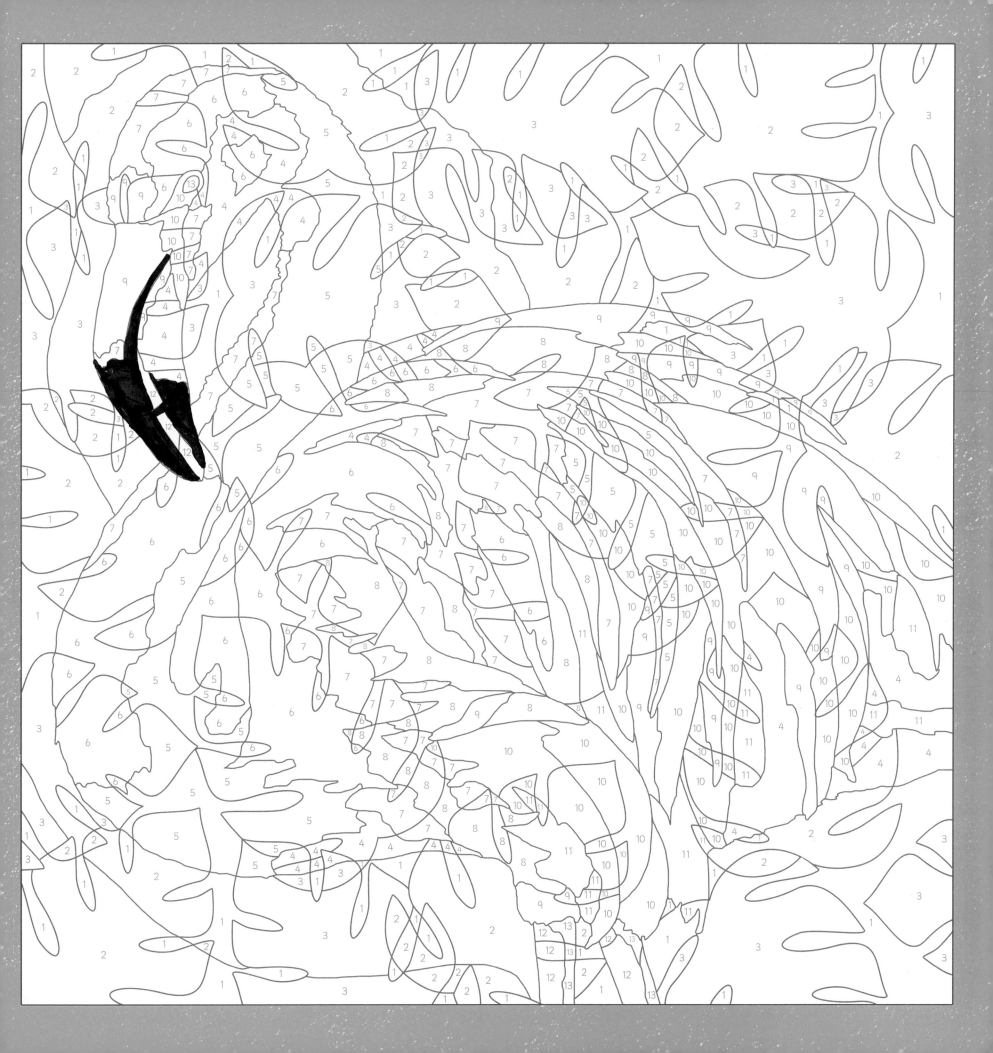

POWERFUL PREDATOR

I am the largest wild cat in the world. I can weigh up to 794 lb (360 kg)— that's about ten of you!

Unlike most other cats, I like the water. I'm a good swimmer and love to cool off in streams and lakes during the heat of the day.

The pattern on my fur camouflages me at night as I creep among the grasses in search of prey.

I live in Asia. Some of my subspecies include Amur, Malayan, Sumatran, and Bengal.

WHAT AM I?

....

TIME: ....

1
2
3
4
5
6
7
8
9
10
11
12

FLOWER POWER

I am a water plant with beautiful, cup-shaped flowers. I rise above the water on thick stalks.

One of my species is called "sacred" and is found in tropical Asia and Australia. The colors of my petals are usually pink or white.

In some parts of Asia, my stalks are fried and sliced as chips, and my leaves are boiled to flavor tea.

In the Buddhist and Hindu religions, I symbolize enlightenment and purity.

WHAT AM I?

....

1
2
3
4
5
6
7
8
9
10
11
12

TIME: ....

MAKING TRACKS

1
2
3
4
5
6
7
8
9
10
11
12

I whiz through cities, the countryside, along mountain sides, and deep under ground. The fastest I can travel is a speedy 374 miles (603 km) per hour.

I have been a popular form of transportation since the 19th century.

Back in the 1800s, my different parts included a firebox, piston, cylinders, and a steam pipe.

I used to be powered by coal or wood, but now I mostly run on diesel or electricity.

WHAT AM I?

....

TIME: ....

CHANGING COLORS

I'm a tree-dwelling lizard with a long tail and grasping feet that hold tightly onto branches.

My eyes move separately to each other, so I can look around for prey without moving my head.

My skin can change color depending on my body temperature or how I'm feeling. If I'm frightened or angry, I may change from green to yellow.

In less than a second, I can shoot out my sticky tongue, snatch an insect, and snap it back in again.

WHAT AM I?

....

TIME: ....

1
2
3
4
5
6
7
8
9
10
11
12

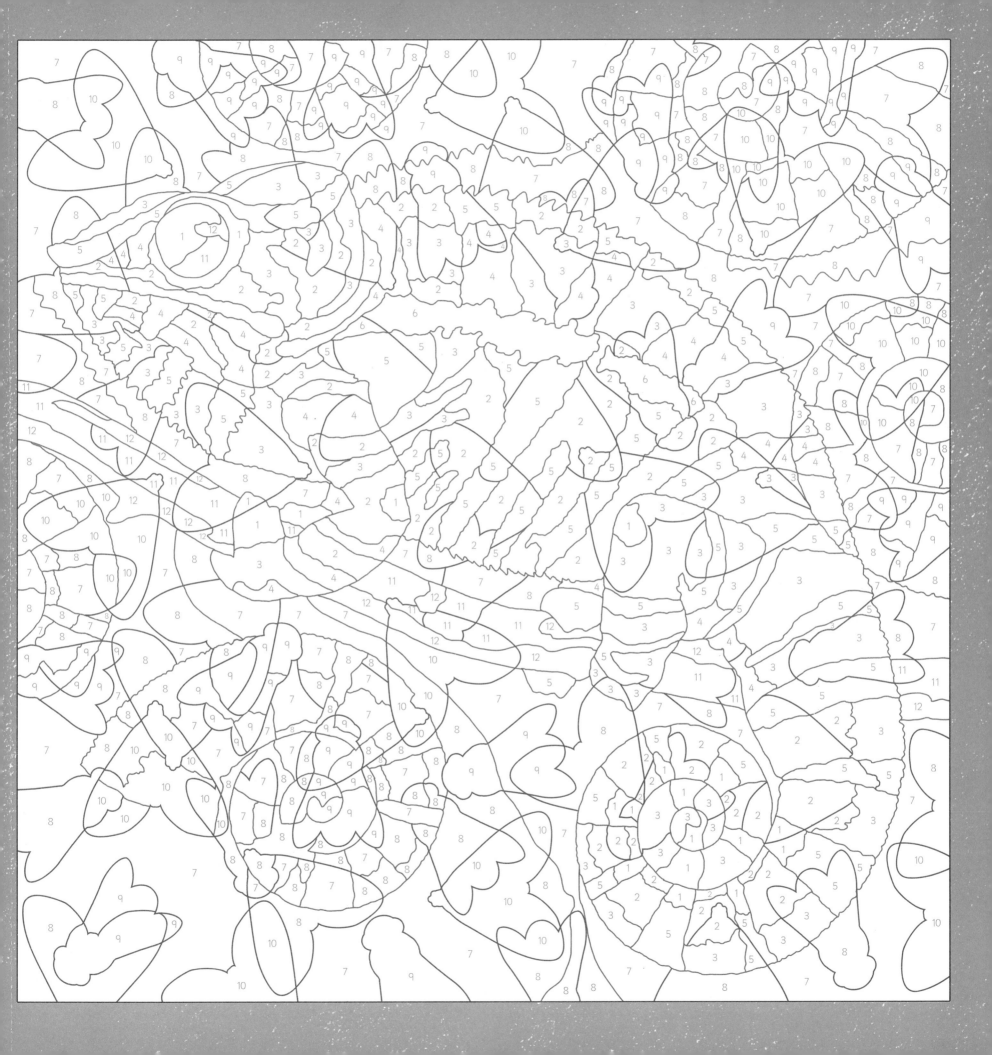

TINY BUT TOUGH

With my short legs and long body, I look like a hot dog, which is how I got my nickname.

My name means "badger dog" in German. I was originally bred to hunt badgers and other tunneling animals, such as foxes.

I make a loving, playful pet. I like to be the center of attention and need plenty of cuddles.

I might be small but I'm also tough and brave. I have large paws for digging and a strong, barrel-like chest.

WHAT AM I?

....

1
2
3
4
5
6
7
8
9
10
11
12

TIME: ....

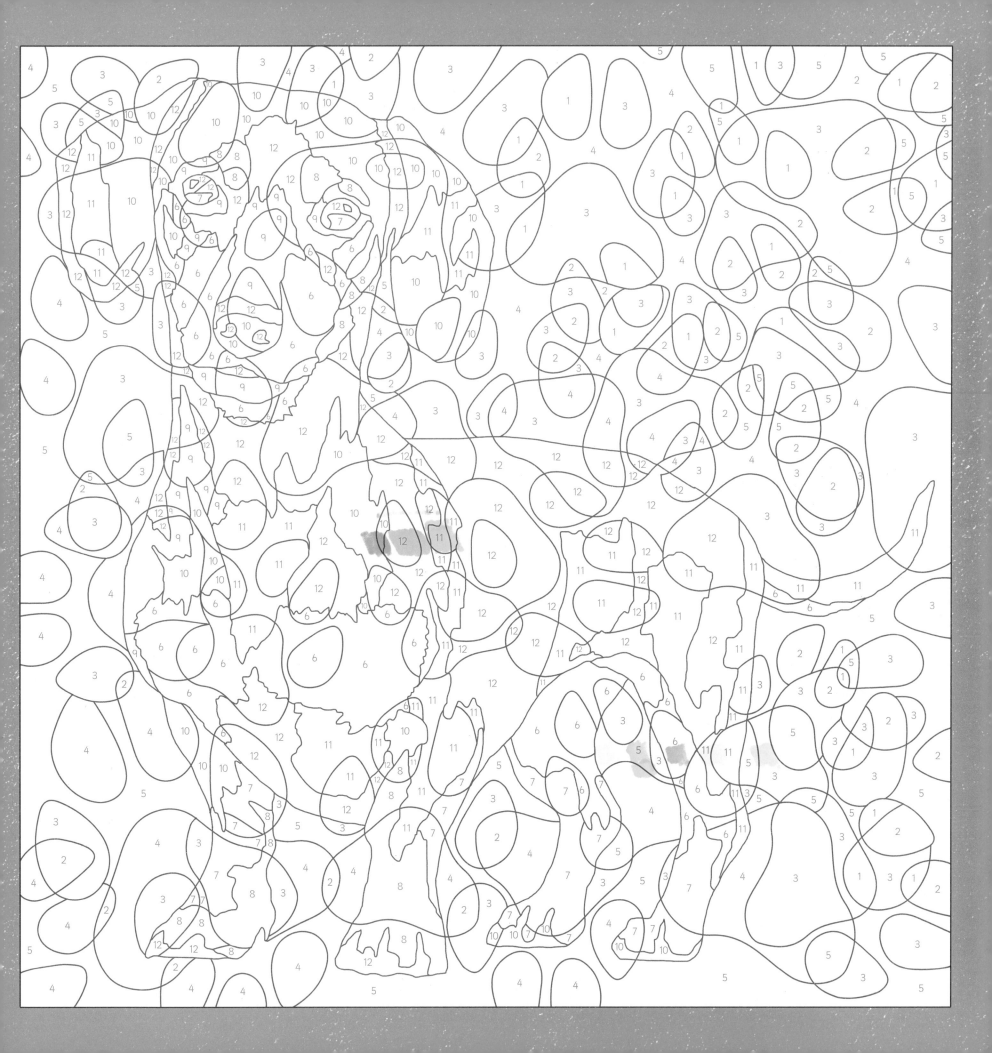

EXTREME PUZZLE 13

BEAUTIFULLY BRIGHT

My squawks can be heard echoing through the Amazonian canopy. I use my calls to communicate with others in my flock.

I use my strong toes to climb through the branches of my rainforest home.
215 /3   130 /1   154 /1

My brightly colored feathers make me harder to spot among the colorful forest trees.
197 195   187 /4   19 -/8

My beak is so powerful that I can easily crack nuts and seeds with it in one crunch.

WHAT AM I?

....

TIME: ....

FINE FORTRESS

1
2
3
4
5
6
7
8
9
10

Within my walls you might find a great hall, solar, keep, and bailey. You may also once have seen pages, jesters, and minstrels.

I am made from stone or wood. My walls and towers are tall and strong to protect against attackers.

I am the fortified home of a king or lord who lived hundreds of years ago.

Many of us were built during the Middle Ages, between the 5th and 15th centuries, around Europe and the Middle East.

WHAT AM I?

....

TIME: ....

PAINTED LADY

I am always beautifully presented, with neat hair, exquisite clothes, and delicate make-up.

I perform tea ceremonies in a special building called a tea house.

I wear a traditional Japanese gown called a kimono, embroidered with detailed patterns.

I am an expert at singing, dancing, and poetry. In Japanese, my name means "art person."

WHAT AM I?

....

224

TIME: ....

TALL TOWER

2
3
4
5
7
8
9
10
11

I am a tower-like structure made of stone, wood, or brick. I have many levels and a curved roof.

I was built mainly for religious worship, or for storing precious sacred objects.

I am mostly found in the countries of Eastern and Southeastern Asia, such as India, China, and Japan.

I am sometimes used as a decorative building in gardens and parks.

WHAT AM I?

....

TIME: ....

COOL AND CAMOUFLAGED

You will find me in the grasslands and treeless savannas of Eastern and Southern Africa.

Each of us has a unique pattern of stripes, much like your fingerprints. Underneath my dazzling stripes, my skin is actually all black.

As an herbivore, I love to munch on the local flora of my home, such as grass, shrubs, and even young trees.

Being a member of the horse family, I communicate through braying and neighing.

WHAT AM I?

....

TIME: ....

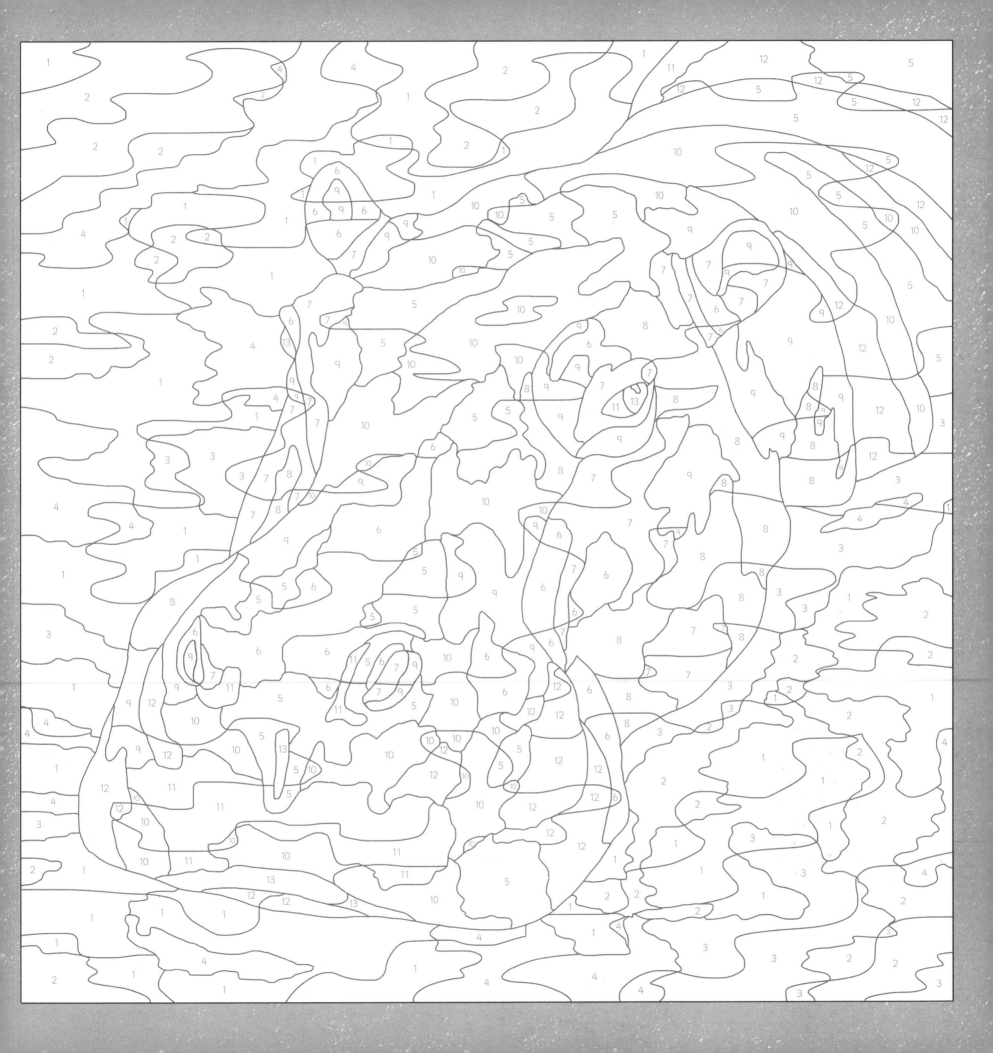

SNAP, SNAP!

1
2
3
4
5
6
7
8
9
10
11
12
13

I am not a crocodile or an alligator, but I belong to a group of reptiles called crocodilians. My name means "alligator" in Spanish.

You'll find me in Central and South America, lurking in groups along riverbanks and swamps.

I am usually smaller than my alligator and crocodile relatives, but my bite is just as fierce.

I have a long, rounded snout, beady eyes, and a huge tail. My jaw is powerful to help me kill my prey, such as fish, birds, and small animals.

WHAT AM I?

....

TIME: ....

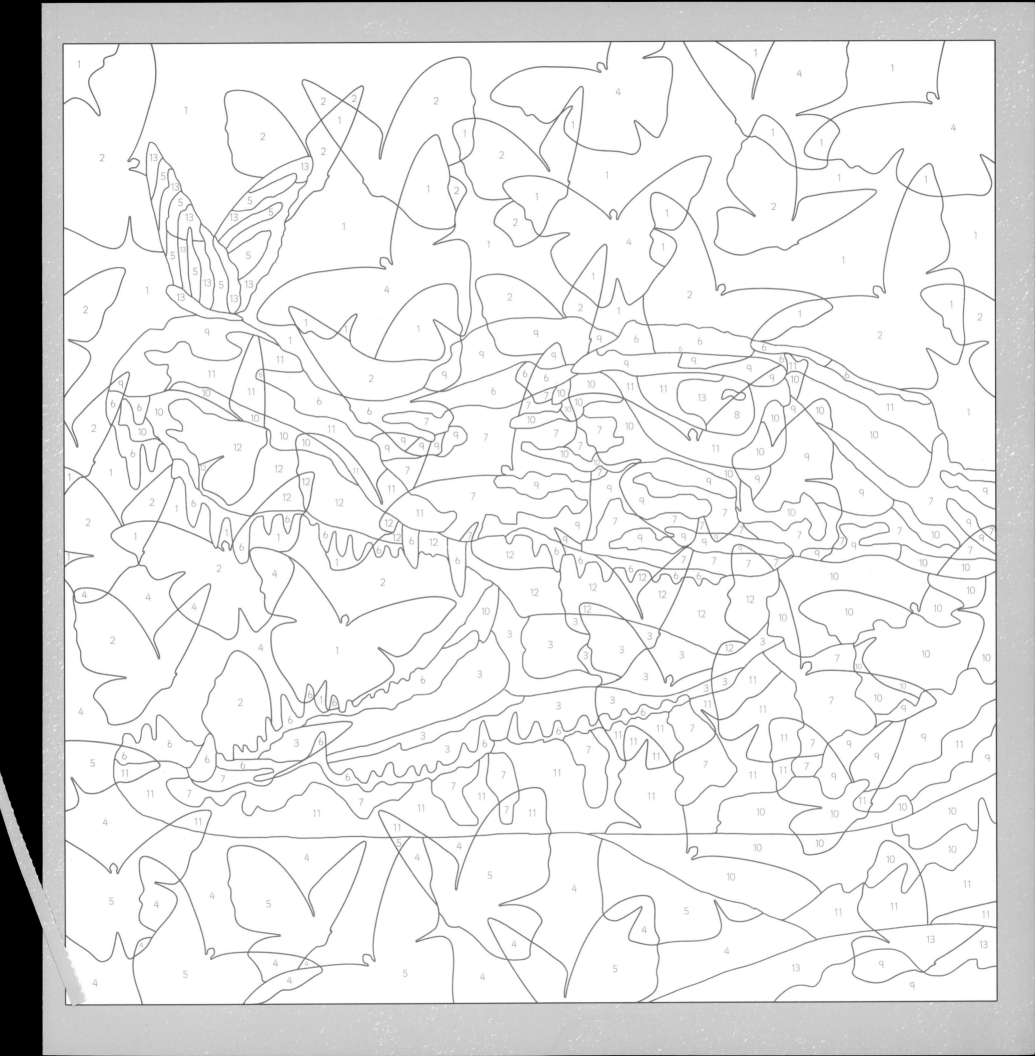

FURRY FRIEND

1
2
3
4
5
6
7
8
9
10
11

I'm a small, furry rodent, also known as a cavy. I have a rounded body, short legs, and no tail.

I come from the grasslands of South America, where I was first bred by humans for food. Now I make a popular pet.

I "chat" with my friends using all sorts of sounds, including squeaks, chirps, whistles, and purrs.

I don't come from the country in my name, and I'm not related to the animal my name suggests.

WHAT AM I?

....

TIME: ....

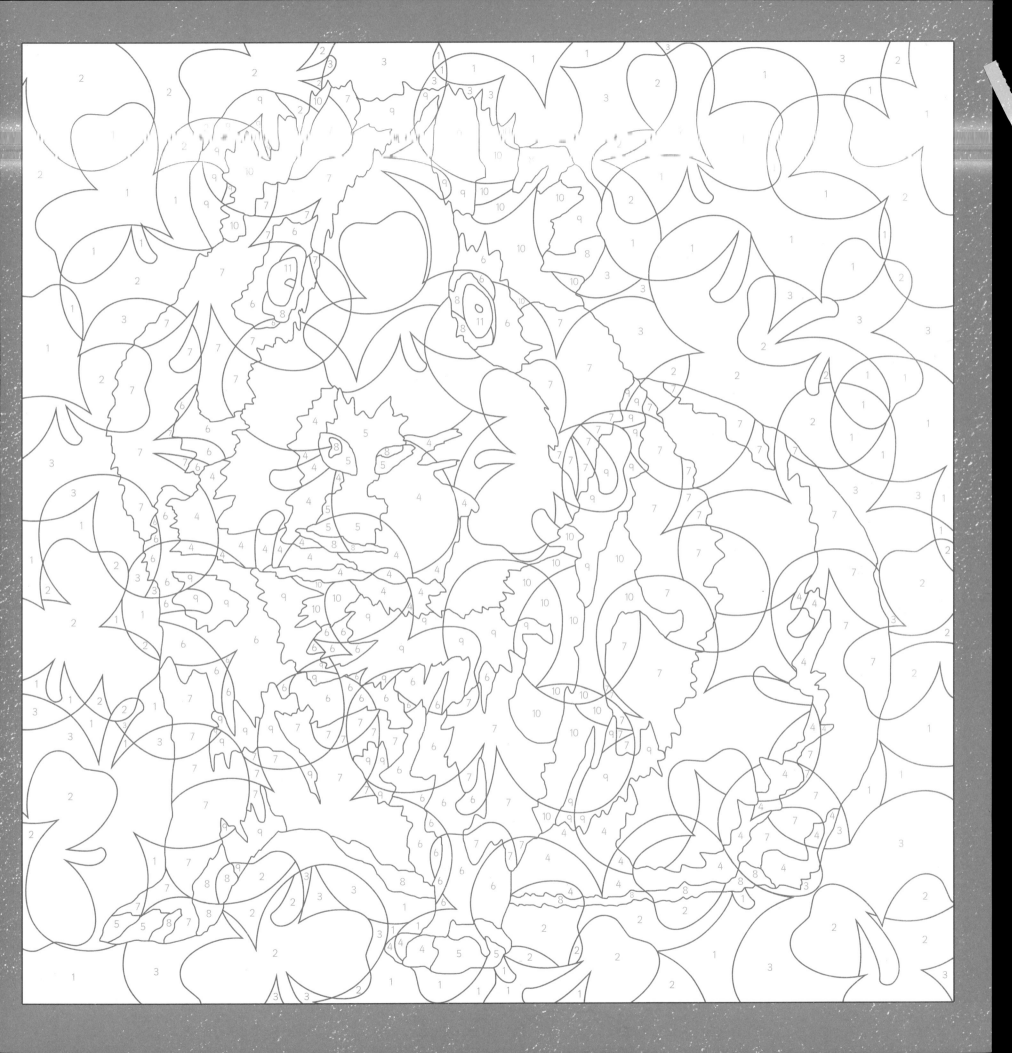

SMALL AND SPINY

I might not look like one, but I'm actually a fish. I am named for the unusual shape of my head.

My body is covered in tiny, spiny plates. I use my curved tail to grip onto sea plants to wait for passing prey.

To keep me safe from predators, I'm a master of camouflage. I can quickly change my color to match my surroundings.

I'm the only animal species on Earth whose male gives birth to the young.

WHAT AM I?

....

1
2
3
4
5
6
7
8
9
10
11
12
13
14

TIME: ....

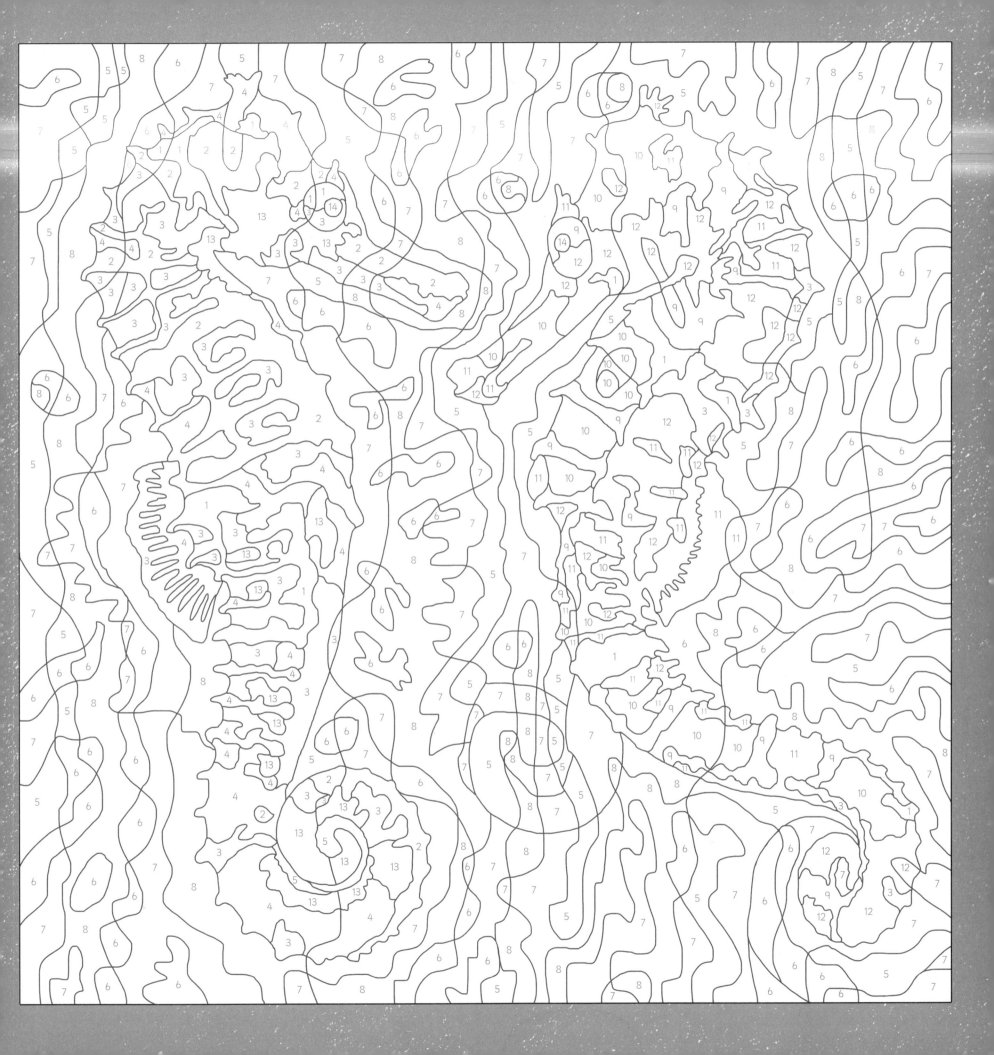

ON THE ROAD

1
2
3
4
5
6
7
8
9
10
11
12
13
14

For more than 130 years, I have been giving people the freedom to travel where and when they like.

My first gas-powered model traveled at a top speed of 9.9 mph (16 km/h). Now, I can reach speeds of over 270 mph (435 km/h).

I am made mostly from steel, aluminum, and plastic. My different parts include a hood, engine, fuel tank, and exhaust pipe.

I am an important means of transportation for emergency services, such as the police and paramedics.

WHAT AM I?

....

TIME: ....

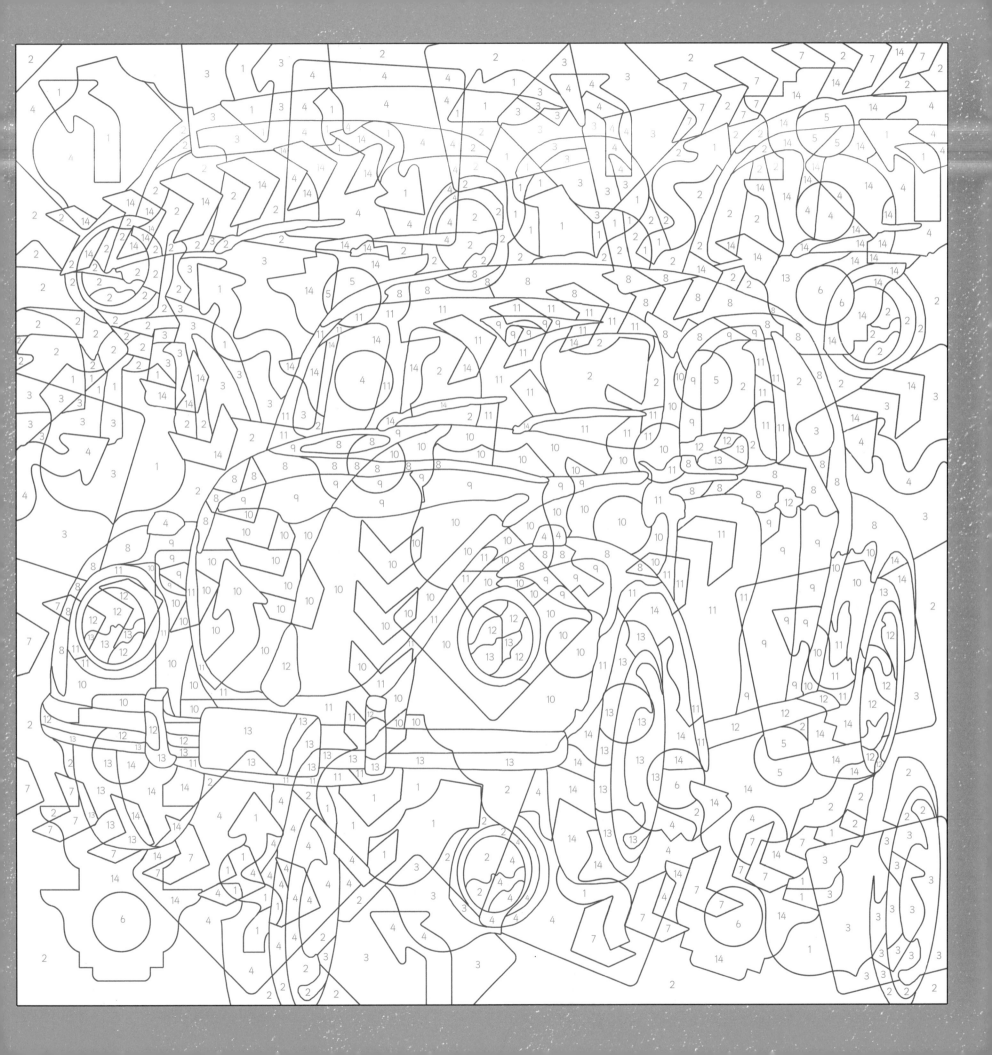

SEEING SPOTS

1
2
3
4
5
6
7
8
9
10
11

With my beautiful spotted coat, long whiskers, and tail, I am easy to recognize.

I am strong enough to drag prey twice my size up into the trees, where I can keep it hidden from other predators.

You'll find me in Africa and Asia, but my numbers are decreasing in the wild, due to deforestation and hunting.

I like to spend my time up in the trees. Hidden by the leaves, I can stalk my prey from above, then pounce!

WHAT AM I?

....

TIME: ....

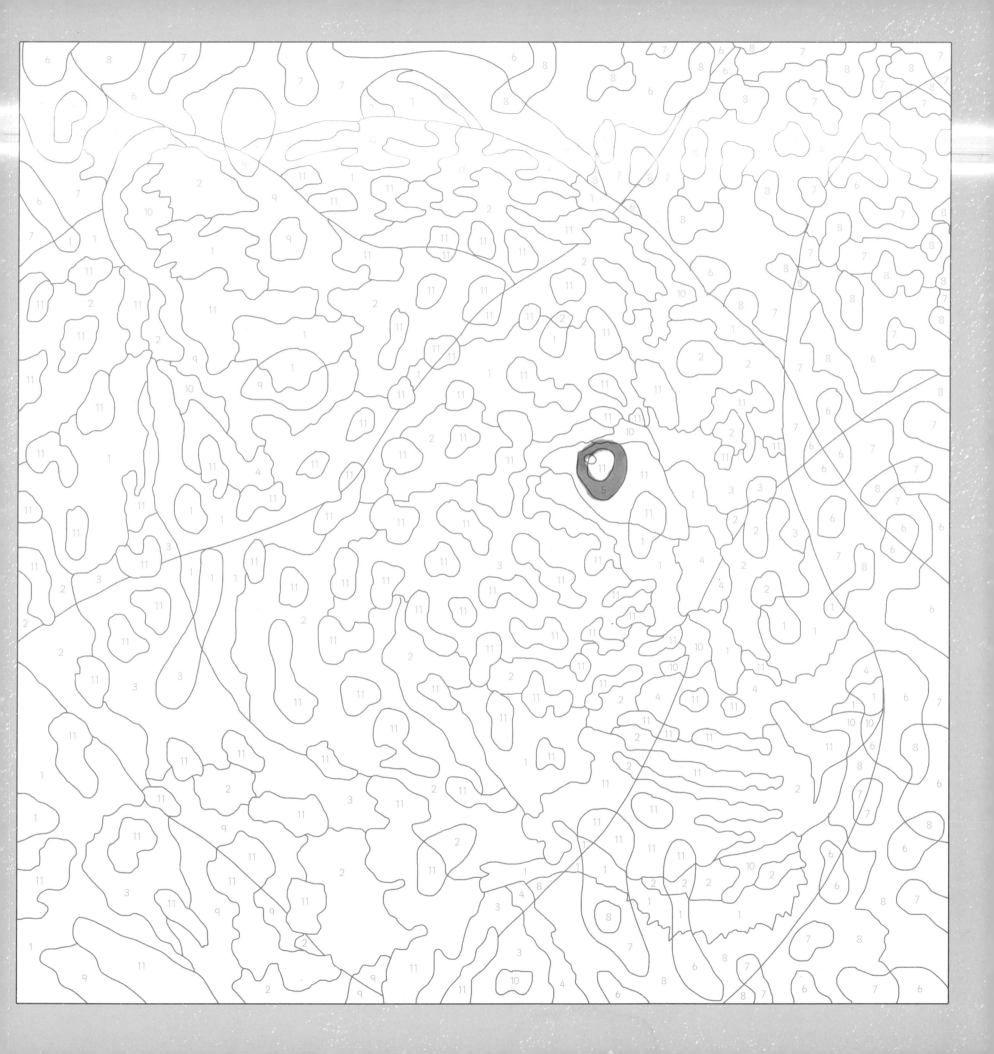

CUTE CLIMBER

I live in the foothills of the Himalayan mountains in Asia, where I spend most of my time up in the trees.

I am about the size of a large pet cat, with rust-colored fur and special claws that help me climb skillfully from tree to tree.

Scientists used to think I was a kind of bear or raccoon, but now they say I'm not closely related to any other animal.

Like another animal of a similar name, my favorite food is bamboo. I'll also happily munch on insects, fruit, and birds' eggs.

WHAT AM I?

....

1
2
3
4
5
6
7
8
9
10
11
12

TIME: ....

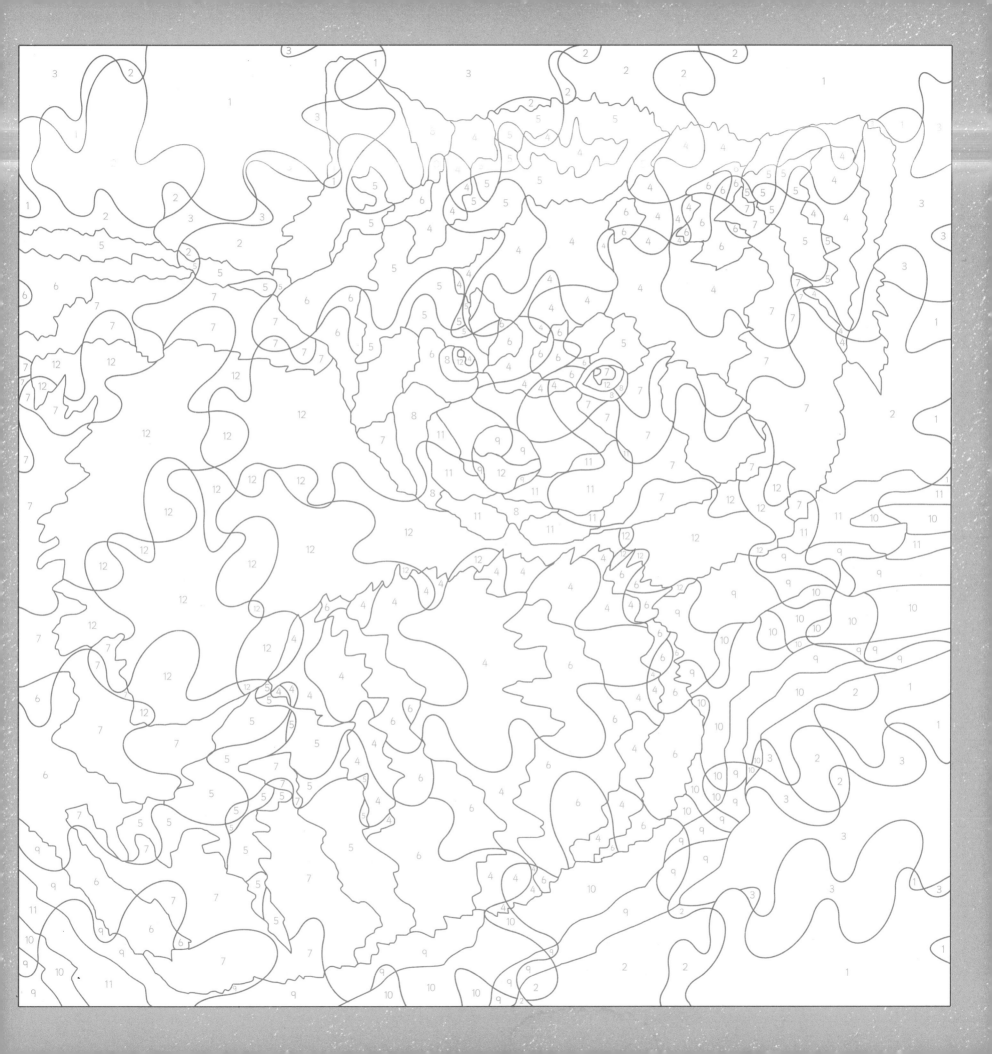

BILLIONS OF BUGS

The group of insects to which I belong is the largest in the world. Out of every three insects, one will be like me.

I have long, delicate flying wings that fold up beneath a pair of tough, hard outer wings.

There are around 400,000 species of me. I'm found all over the world in different types of habitats, from rainforests to deserts.

My size varies greatly. I can be as tiny as a period or as large as an adult's hand.

WHAT AM I?

....

1

2

3

4

5

6

7

8

9

10

11

12

13

TIME: ....

HIGH FLYERS

1
2
3
4
5
6
7
8
9
10
11
12
13

My first successful launch was in 1903 by the Wright brothers. I stayed in the air for 59 seconds.

My different parts include the fuselage, cockpit, wheels, and propellers.

I have a tail and wings, but I'm not a bird.

I vary in size, and can be as small as a school bus or as large as eight buses put together.

WHAT AM I?

....

TIME: ....

SCUTTLE AND SHUFFLE

I belong to a group of animals called decapods, which means "ten legs." Others in my group include prawns and shrimps.

There are around 7,000 species of me throughout the world. Many of us have funny names, such as hermit, spider, robber, ghost, and fiddler.

I use my sharp pincers for catching and picking apart my prey. I also use them for fighting off predators.

As I grow, my hard shell begins to split open and fall off. The new, softer shell underneath expands before it hardens.

WHAT AM I?

....

1
2
3
4
5
6
7
8
9
11
12

TIME: ....

THE ANSWERS

1 CLOWN FISH

2 OWL

3 SATURN

4 SQUIRREL

5 OCTOPUS

6 FLAMINGO

7 TIGER

8 KINGFISHER

9 LOTUS FLOWER

10 TRAIN

11 CHAMELEON

12 DACHSHUND (HOT DOG)

13 PARROT

14 CASTLE

15 COCKATIEL

16 GEISHA

17 OTTER

18 PAGODA

19 ZEBRA

20 HIPPOPOTAMUS

21 CAIMAN

22 GUINEA PIG

23 SEAHORSE

24 CAR

25 LEOPARD

26 RED PANDA

not done

27 BEETLE

28 AIRPLANE

29 CRAB